The Melodies Of Silence

By

Olusheyi A. Banjo

Foreword

This book is actually my tenth anniversary poetry book. I still cannot believe the my first book "In Sorrow And Song" was published ten years ago. Life has taken me through many things, many up and some downs since the publishing of that book. This book is a celebration of everything that life has given me in the last two years or so since "Galactic Underground" was published.This book also is a kind of sequel to "In Sorrow And Song", hence the title. As in the previous books, I give the reader a look into my soul and my state of mind.As well as my views of the world events that have gone on. This book also has a fun side, I put a hip hop poem in the book as well as a silly rhyming poem. This book also has a sweet love side to it as well, I talk about the love ups and downs that I been through as well.I have also included my very first Spanish language poem "Amour Fresco' as well as another nigerian poem. This book is about my life and my melodies. Enjoy reading it.

Acknowledgements

First and foremost, I give all praise and glory to the most high God,for giving me the strength to do another book.Lord without you absolutely none of these poems would be possible.Thank you for loving me. Thank you to my wonderful mother and stepfather.I appreciate your wholehearted prayers.To my big sister Olubunmi, thank you for having my back when I need you, our song "We're gonna Make It" is awesome.To my big brother Olusegun,God bless bro, We will speak soon.

My wonderful grandmother Patricia and my dynamic grandfather Luke,no one could ask for better grandparents.I love you both.To my aunts,uncles and cousins around the world,thank you for being a great family to me.Grandma Flo,your motivation is priceless.My Godfather Benjamin Williams,I love you man so much.Godmother Saundra Royster,love you always.Thank youto my awesome church family Grant AME in Long Beach & Pastor Michael Eagle Sr., God bless all of you. To my triple O family,(Ronin Gray, Wicked Rob & Lil Gee), God bless you all. You all are awesome. Julius,the most wonderful best friend that any man could ask for. Thank you for listening to my drama.Thank you Tim & Becky Baumgarner. Thank you Michael Gonzalez for being a real friend and accepting me for myself. Thank you Micaal,Thank you Dante Mitchell. Thank you ROK, Thank you Bobby Bucjk, the best manager anyone could ask for,Thank you Geza X. Thank you Erik Sarni. Thank you Tim Poole, you are so funny & you are a mess.lol.Thank you David Cipres Jr. Thank you Joey Herman. Thank you Tom Hicks. Thank you Unkal Bean.Thank you Brenton Fosner and Gilbert Mscorro. Thank you Cornerstone Theatre Company, Thank you Ron,Juan. Thank you Skid Row 3 on 3. Thank you Choko. Thank you Skid Row Housing Trust. Thank you David Andrews. Thank you Deon Joseph. You are an awesome friend. Thank you Devonte & Myesha James. Thank You Kirk Milton Jr.Thank you Barbara Farley.Thank you Lashaun Jones.Thank you Brain Smith.Thank you Marco Winfrey.Thank you to everyone at

BethanY Christian Bible College in Los Angeles.Thank you Robert Foreman.Thank you Erik Sarni & Robert Amaya.Hobbfase and Griemy lvoe y'all. Thank you Arend Beal. Young Shame & Killa Cane.James Rachal, you are an awesome man, may God continue to bless you.

Dedication

This book is dedicated to my Father,Festus Adeeko Banjo,my great grandmother, Juanita Robinson,Sharon Williams, Mary Floyd Hawkins,Tabitha Anthony,Rev.James Bobo,Clifford Rheda, Walt, Uncle Clevester Donaldson.I will always remember and love you. This book is also dedicated to my wonderful godson Devonte Deon James 3.Your Godfather loves you man.I know you grow up to be a wonderful man.Remember,I got your back always.Also to my godchildren, John and Joseph, you will be awesome young men. I love you both.

#1(poem)

We are #1, we won't stop
We are #1,we won't drop
#1 in rapping,singing, living and loving
#1 yes we are born to do this
Doesn't matter if time passes us by
You know who loves you
We do
We are all black and all that
and we will forever be #1

I Win Again(poem)
Oh you tried to write me off
but I win again
Called me all kinds of names
but,I win again
Told me defeat was in my future's path
but,I win again
I am a warrior, a conqueror,a winner of it all
Defeated never
I keep getting better
I win because I am a winner
I win
I win
and I win again
(inspired by Still I Rise by Maya Angelou)

Untitled (Poem)
I present you the fruit of my love,but you, refuse it
I bring you the best of my harvest,but you laugh in my face
I bow myself to you
But you kick me down
Why do I give,live,love you when you're not the one

When Jesus Calls Me Home (a poem for Sharon Williams)
When Jesus calls me home
What a day of rejoicing it will be
I will lay down the troubles and pains of this life
I will dance, sing & shout the victory
I made it over, made it to my heavenly rest
Hallelujah I past all of this life's test
My living was not in vain, I lived the life of a true christian,
A child of the most high God
Unspeakable joy will overflow in my soul
When Jesus calls me home

Life Keeps Goin' On(poem)
Sure i'm lonely,of course I miss you
But my life keeps goin' on
Yeah i'm jealous that most of my friends have somebody
But my life keeps goin' on
Sure I'm getting everything material back
And life keeps goin' on
As sure as this world keeps turnin
And God is still on the throne
I will find a new love
Until then,my life keeps going on

*Betrayal(A Poem for an enemy) *
I should act a fool,but I'll let the court deal with you
You're nothing but a thief
Stole my money,stole my time, stole from the innocent kids.
How can you look yourself in the mirror daily knowing you stabbed a friend
in the back.
Trusted you with bringing my song to visual light.
But little did I know that you weren't right
Go on man have your fun,laugh while you can.
Cause I will have the last laugh.
See you in court scoundrel

World Outside My Window (poem)
Looking out my beautiful window I see this world as it truly is
On my right side I see the beauty of humanity
The green grass,the trees,the city,the love that people show
On my left,homelessness and poverty
Hate and desparation
I want to hang my head
In the middle,I see what life should be
A hope for eternity
A tall strong blessed filled reality
I see these things when I gaze out my window

Mine All Mine(poem)
It may not be the Taj Mahal
But it's mine all mine
It may not compare to Buckingham Palace
But I love it just the same
May not be The White House
May not tower over the city,may not be in the best area
But i'm content with it
Cause when I close my door,I have peace
It is my oasis from this crazy world
My place to create,my home sweet home
It's wonderful to me
I'm happy this place is mine,all mine

Desperation (poem)
I thirst for you like a man in the desert
Long to feel a lovers touch once more
To kiss to hold to go to that wonderfully special place
My choices for love have betrayed my heart
Have cast the feeling assunder
Out of desperation,i have done unruly things
Oh how I wish that I could change this desperation into a love flower
A beautiful rose
But for now I am bound by my wrong love choices

Oluvation(poem)
Sometimes I'm heavy
Most times I'm light
Overall I'm outta sight
& alright
On this journey a travelin' I go
Damn I love being big O

Langston,Maya&Me(poem)
Langston Maya & me
Three generations of poetry
Langston brought the Harlem Renaissance to life
The jazz poetry & the world's plights
Maya brought the soul & pride of peoplehood
Her work is deep and connects with the soul
Still I rise and here we go
I'm bringing the hip-hop,the gospel flava & the urban life
Putting up a screen to 21 century life
Me & Proud To Be,In Sorrow & Song
Hip-pop poetry,all season long
Langston,Maya & Me
Three generations of outstanding poetry

Hip-Pop Poem(2012)(poem)
Call me maybe,I'll be your boyfriend
I'll give you diamonds,make you numb
Can't stand this heart attack,one more night
Doin' it gangnam style
We are never ever getting back together if we live while we're young.
I still wanna pop that,no lie
You got me saying,mercy ,turn on the lights
I ain't apart of no clique in a white dress
Lately,I just wanna dance for you,while you adorn
On your feet,cause this is the climax

Someday My Prince Will Come(a poem)
He doesn't have to ride a white horse or have a BMW
He doesn't have to be a superman nor a dark knight
He's just gotta love me right
Gotta give, not take
Can't be a flake
Or a dl fake
He is all mine,don't have to share
We love,we care,we are there
For each other
One day,someday that fairytale love will come true
He will give the kiss of life 2 this dying heart
We will live happily ever after
Oh someday,I know my prince will come

*Let's Get Nasty(an erotic poem) *

We kiss passionately

Desire takes over you,envelopes me.

Let's tear each others clothes off.

I want you to fuck me hard,don't do it soft. Before you do that I want to

suck your cock,& you suck mine.

We'll have a nasty freaky 69.

I take you into my mouth,your precum tastes like a rocky road ice cream

cone.

I love to hear both of us moan.

in the unison of pleasure

Ooh this feeling no one will measure.

I know that I'm ready to feel your cock inside me.

Damn baby make me your bitch.

I want you to fuck me until I scream and my voice is gone.

Fuck me like a mad man or a sex criminal.

I don't want to walk straight for a couple of days.

Give it to me,do it now.

Aaaaah yes daddy.

You're making me wanna climb the walls.

You're making me scream your name.

Talk dirty to me I love it. After awhile,you moan,loudly. I know you're

about 2 cum take it out and spread your cream on my body. Oh how I love it

when we get nasty.

My First Summer Love(poem)
No one else can hold a candel to you
No one else since has totally loved me like you
I close my eyes and reminise
Of the joy your kiss gave to me
Your love was amazing
Had others since you,but they couldn't match our body,mind & soul connection.
It's a shame that our love had to end with the season
But I will never forget you my first summer love

The Melodies Of Silence (poem)
These are the melodies that I hear when I'm alone
By myself
When depression threatens to overwhelm my soul
When my body is too weak
To utter a word,I cannot speak
I look up to the ceiling
Trying to find a good feelin'
But instead
All there is silence
The joyful melodies of my silence

So What (poem)

You say you don't approve of the way I live my life
So what
You say that I'll going straight to hell
So what
You laugh and call me names
So what
Say I'm a square
So what
Talk mess behind my back
So what
Try to use me
So What
Who cares what you think
Cause while you're trying to set me up for a fall
get ready to trip
Get ready to sink like the Titanic ship
You may be the coolest,think you're the best and such
I say
So what
In this crazy world that don't amount to much

Real(poem)
All my friends say I finally got a prize
& for once I agree
God did it finally
blessed me with someone who's driven to success
Just like me
Yet who loves & reassures me
Oh your kiss is magical
Let's me be my wonderful self
whose not about my wealth
a friend a lover a road dog for sure
You're realness is all that & more

*Simple Poem To the KKK *

You say you hate the blacks and the Jew
What is really wrong with you
If you hate us you must hate Jesus Christ too
Cause everyone knows that he was a Jew
Also you must hate Adam & Eve cause they were from Africa,modern day Iran
and Gaza as well
Let that crazy thinking sail
It's not 1950 it's 2013
Get your mind right,make it clean
WAKE UP before it's too late
Wake up and stop this crazy hate

Booty Wood 2(poem)
You can front all you want you to
But you know how you became a superstar
How you got the money for them fancy cars
Front to the public but I , your movie & record producer, manager, record
company exec
Know how you got that paycheck
You had to bend over
Had to give it up
or had to let me have your body
Let me get my fill
You & I know what you have to do to make it
in Bootywood

Justice For Travon & All the Young Black Men(poem)
Their blood is calling to me as I walk down the street
Their missed chances to live a good life,grieves me
It vexes my spirit,hits me in my soul
No way that they can be doctors,lawyers or whatever they chose to be
It's unfair that haters rule this land
I demand justice
Justice for all the murdered young black
We can't let their killers run free
We have to tell on their killers
Send them all to the electric chair
Cause if we don't the animals will continue until all the young black men
are dead
And our race has no future of prosperity
Why is that we protest a white man getting off, but we are scared to tell
when we see another young black man killing his brother
WAKE UP People
Stop being scared & tell the truth
We need justice for all young black men

Let's Get Nasty 2(poem)
I love to put your tits in my mouth
I love to go down south
& eat you like a hungry man dinner
I want us to do a freaky 69
You suck my dick,while on your pussy I dine
No baby don't make me cum yet
Let me lick you some more to get you fully wet
Now it's time for us to fuck
"Aww shucks"
You moan as I stick it in
I love when you talk dirty
I'm groaning,your moaning as we continue on this erotic journey
We visit the erotic valley's, sail on the erotic sea
Oooh wee baby
There's nothing like this in the world
As we prepare for landing, prepare to climax
Baby I can't hold back
I gotta cum and so do you
"Oooooh aaaaah"
This sexual adventure was the best by far

Word Play 8(Andrae Crouch songs) (poem)
I've got the best so I don't bother looking for you
Soon and very soon I'll be heaven bound because Jesus is lord
It's all because of jesus so let the church say amen
I'll be thinking of you lord while I pray & that's the promise that I will
keep
I say yes lord and thank you for everything
The blood will never loose it's power because he's everywhere
I'll keep on singin' because i've got confidence
I don't know why Jesus loves me so i'll take a little time to give him my
tribute in praises

*Motivational Reality (poem) *
I wonder sometimes why is it so hard
So hard to live your positive dreams.
You have 2 go through
Go through so many nightmares 2 achieve 1 part of your dream.
Seems so many haters & jealous folks try 2 stop it
But I know it's going 2 be worth it
In the end

Sweet Reality(poem)
I love sweets
that's why I love you
you're my candy boo
If I stay around you for 2 long
I think I might catch diabetes

Better Not Look Down(poem)
Sometimes it's so hard to smile,with all the drama going on
but
You better not look down
With people loving you 1 day & hating you the next
But
You better not look down
It seems everyone elses dreams are coming true, but all you have is nightmares
But
You better not look down
Even when it seems hard to find a smile, or keep your head up,
Still
You better not look down
For the next day will bring the sunshine that you seek
Keep flying,even if you have to dip a bit
Just don't look down
Don't give up
Cause when you do you will crash.
Keep on my brother,keep flying my sister
Keep it moving,keep going full steam ahead
You better not look down

The Lord Will Make A Way (poem)
This journey sure ain't easy sometimes but I know
The Lord will make a way somehow
So many things to do,yet so little money
But I know
The Lord will make a way somehow
My good is sometimes evil spoken of
But I know
The Lord will make a way somehow
He will do it in his own time
He will work it out better than I ever could
He will make things all 2 the good
I have tried him and I know no matter what it looks like right now
The Lord will make a way somehow
No Rhyme No Reason(poem)
I offered my body & you took it from
me
In sweet estacy
The feeling had me high & gliding
I didn't it to end
But it had to my friend
Then you tried to ask me to give up my dollars
I wanted to scream out,I wanted to hollar
I also found out that you had others
Came with a lame excuse
& because of the passion,I bought it
I wish I didn't fall for the passion.
I wish you didn't let you in
Conquered my will with your game
I feel lame
But I would do it again
You awakened my inner freaky side

I fell in love with you
But I realize that love has no rhyme or reason
It just is

Can't Believe You Knew(poem)
All this time,thought I was hiding from you
Can't believe you knew
All these years you could tell
Can't believe you knew
Tried to keep my feelings covered up
Can't believe you knew
You knew how I really felt for you
But you knew & you waited for me to tell you my feelings
Can't believe you knew that I really love you

Ms. Bwould(poem)
Gettin' my groove on in my favorite club
Dancing without a care
Saw Ms. B
Ms. Bwould 2 be exact
Hips of a goddess and a great face and body to match
Played it nonchanant
She knew that it was what I want
Walk over and a conversation did ensue
The conversation was as beautiful as the sweetest hue
As the night progressed we danced endless times
We made plans for another song
Knew that it was on
Her cellphone rang
Said she had to go
No explaination did she offer
Just disappeared into the crowd
Tried to follow
But to no avail
Now my heart feels like I failed

* Depression(poem)*
Even though, it's sunny outside
It's raining in my heart
This feeling is deplitating
Feels so lonely
Like i'm in the desert
No oasis in sight
The light is dim
It is completely dark when you are depressed

Classy(Poem)
I carry myself with class
which lets them know i'm not just a piece of ass
Some think i'm crass
But I tell them like it is
Don't come at me with drama
Cause my door you won't get past
All that & more
That's how it is when your too classy for trash

Imagination(poem)
I close my eyes and I imagine what it would be like
If we were together
As a couple
It probably be heaven
Pure heaven on earth
Every day would be a special day
Even if we argue, I would still love you
I wish that we could make my imagination come true

* In The Sky(poem)*
I saw a new star in the sky tonight
Shining ever so beautiful & ever so bright
It shined on me like the sun
Even though i'm sure it was seen by everyone
In my heart, I knew it was you,Travon W.
shining your brightness on me, 1 more time
Though you're not here on earth,
I know that I can look up to the sky
and feel your love shining forevernore

No Greater Love (Poem)
To lay down you life for your friend
that's no greater love
To give of yourself unselfishly
that's no greater love
To smile, at people, even when they hate on you
that's no greater love
Unconditional, pure, giving with no ulterior motive
that's no greater love
real love is shown & proved
that's what I call no greater love

Follow The Script(poem)
I am strong & not weak
I am fighter
I follow the script of life
I never try to deviate
Cause this stage play called life is sometimes a comedy,sometimes a drama
But in the end, I hope to gain a standing ovation from my creator

Everybody Wants To Be A Star (poem)
I've been to New York,even lived on Skid Row
And I noticed this 1 thing
Everybody wants to be a star
No matter how you try to deny it
Everybody wants the spotlight
Some go outta their way to be the star
Some are just unbearable with their quest for fame
Some go about it the wrong way
Some go about it the right
Some are dedicated to being their very best
They reach for the top in everything that they do
I've been far, I've been wide
but I learned
Everyone has a need to be a star

Love's Dance(poem)
I put my hand in your hand
Let you lead me
Lead me in this dance
This dance called love
Surrender my attitude,my reservation
My preconcieved notions
Let you hold me close
As we move across the floor
We take our first dip
As we dance,your lips touch my lips
Heaven is what I feel
When we dance,the dance of love
My soul is ignited once more
During' love's dance

Real Anger(Shut This Shit Down)(Poem)
Why should I fight
for a government where I am less than human
Why should I pay
To a government where justice is for all, except me
They're content to see me in poverty
So they can kick me and keep me down
So they decided to shut it down, so that I couldn't get anything
How evil can they be
I waisted my time to vote for these modern day slavemasters
This is a first class disaster
Cutting everything that helps
Time for us to be like them & be out for self
We need to protest in these streets
Make them take off their sheets
Time to overthrow the beast
Give it back to the people
Forget the tea party & the crooked ass politicians
They all can go to hell
Time to stand up
Instead of sitting down & being content by what they decide to give us
Just cause they give you a position that don't mean shit
Won't be long before this government goes the way of the roman empire
Oh how great the fall will be for these greedy
you ask me why I don't care
Cause they don't care about me

I've Got A Crush On You(poem)
Haven't told anyone my true feelings
I don"t think they suspect at all
Not even my best friend knows
But I got a crush on you
Stronger it gets every day
I'm just too shy to say
Been through unrequited love, don't wanna go through it again
Been the liker,not the likee
Been called a weird so and so
Oh how I see us happy together
Laughing,loving and sharing together
In my mind, I paint beautiful pictures of us
In my heart, you're the knight in shining armor rescuing me from the loveless desert
In my soul, you are the one
But for now, you don't know that
I've got a crush on you

*Motivation(poem) *
Run on
Fight on
One more step
Climb that latter
Go higher and higher
Walk them steps
Pick up the pace
Time you shouldn't waiste
Because if you stop
You'll never get to the top
Don't give up, don't you quit
Your goal you will achieve
If you just stay motivated

*Joy Floods My Soul(Poem) *
When I think of your love and sacrifice for me Lord
Joy floods my soul
When I think of the gifts and talents you gave for everyone to see
Gratefulness fills my spirit
I think of the life you've chosen for me
Love floods my heart
The assignment you've given me
Hope fills my being
Lord you didn't have to give me anything
You didn't have to set me free
You didn't have to die on Calvary
You could've walked away
That's why joy, gratefulness, love and hope fill my very being

Get On The Ball, Or Don't Do It At All (Poem)
If you're trying to get somewhere or trying to do something great
To you I say "Get on the ball, or don't do it at all"
If you want to do positive things or make your dreams come true
I simply say "Get on the ball, or don't do it at all"
Don't hold back, go for what you know
Don't procrastinate
Do it now,don't wait
For everyday you wait
It might be too late
Don't pay attention to the hate
So I say to the dreamers,the lovers,the creative, the inventive people
Just get on the ball or don't do it at all

Misread (a poem for Ronin)

When I first met you, I thought you were going to be a crazy drama king

You know what I mean

But talking more to you

I discovered you are a deep soul

A soul seeking understanding

A deep soul with knowledge

Plus respect

You're In tune with life

And it's rhythm

This is one time that I misread another person

Be Myself (Poem)
In this crazy world, where fake seems real, and real people fake
All I wanna do is be myself
Folks are scared to be who they are,rather live a lie
I just wanna be myself
Fakin' and shakin' are the norm
I wanna be myself
Don't wanna pretend, just so I can be accepted
Just wanna be myself
The people that I work so hard to impress aren't worth it
Just wanna be myself
Fuck the folks who pretend and talk behind my back
I'm being myself
Opened up to you & you tried to use it against me
Don't wanna be seen with the real me
You can be fake and be a two faced bitch, i'm gonna be real and i'm gonna
be myself
Flaws and all
So go fuck yourself if you can't accept the real me

*Amor Fresco(**(Cool Love)**(poem)*
Tu amor me hace sonreír
(Your love makes me smile)
Porque tienes el amor más es fresco
(Because you love is cool)
Tu amor calma mi alma de una manera especial
(Your love calms my soul in a special way)
Nunca me preocupo cuando esté cerca de
(I never worry when you are near)
No quiero volver a perderte
(I never want to loose you)
Mi vida mi amor mi todo
(my life, my love, my all)
Me siento muy afortunada de tener este amor fresco
(I feel very fortunate to have this cool love)
Me siento fantástico, con este amor fresco
(I feel fantastic, with this cool love)
Gracias a Dios por este amor fresco
(Thank God for this cool love)
Nuestro amor fresco
(Our cool love)

Never Changin' God(poem)
So glad that I serve a never changin' God
You're not fickle
You love me every day that you send
You're mercy for me is everlasting towards me
If they ask me to measure your grace
I simply could not do it
I'm madly in love with you
My never changing God
My everlasting father
My greatest friend
My soul's lover
No heartbreak will you give to me
You give me your joy every day
I love my never changing God
All Is Well(poem)
I know you want to see me sad & giving you a sob story
But i'll simply tell you, all is well
I know you want me to cry the blues
But I say all is well
I know you want me to be miserable
But all is well
Your misery won't get any company from me
Your two faced hatefulness won't stop me
Your fakeness don't effect me
I'll scream it loud, i'll shout it on the mountain
I'll sing it in a song,write it in a poem, or even act it out in a play
All is well, all is well, all is well

Be Myself (Poem)

In this crazy world, where fake seems real, and real people fake
All I wanna do is be myself
Folks are scared to be who they are,rather live a lie
I just wanna be myself
Fakin' and shakin' are the norm
I wanna be myself
Don't wanna pretend, just so I can be accepted
Just wanna be myself
The people that I work so hard to impress aren't worth it
Just wanna be myself
Fuck the folks who pretend and talk behind my back
I'm being myself
Opened up to you & you tried to use it against me
Don't wanna be seen with the real me
You can be fake and be a two faced bitch, i'm gonna be real and i'm gonna
be myself
Flaws and all
So go fuck yourself if you can't accept the real me

Conversationalist(poem)
I love that wherever I go, or whatever I do
I always have someone to talk to
Or someone is always talking to me
Love my friendly, approachable nature
I can make a friend wherever I roam
Love to make nice strangers feel at home
Love to share a smile or even a great laugh
We talk about sports, music, or even Moses and the golden calf
Even when I'm on the train,bus or travelin' elsewhere
Find people talking with me about their cares
Listen and laugh, that's me
I guess you can call me a conversationalist
Yes, i'm a conversationalist through and through

You Fall In Love 2 Quick(Poem)
Just 1 look,just 1 glance
& i'm ready to give my all
Just one flirty message, a sexy sign
& i'm ready to make you mine
Some of my friends tell me
You fall in love 2 quick
Give love time to grow
But I pay them no mind,
I simply tell them have you ever heard of love at first sight
I know this feelin' is so right
But they continue to say Olusheyi, you fall in love 2 quick
Quick love never lasts
But I pay them no mind & continue to love like there's no tomorrow
Love with my whole heart

PTSD(poem)
If you knew the real me would you accept it
If you could see into my soul how would you react
If you knew all of my secrets would you even look at me the same
Some days I feel strong & able to conquer the world
Others, I feel depressed and lonely
Sometimes I say God why me
Why must I go through this mental anguish
But no answer comes
That's when I realize the truth

Expression Of Fantasy(Poem)
I long to feel your lips against my waiting
lips
I hunger for your soothing embrace
I dream of the comfort of your body next to mine
Your touch is as sweet as a chocolate candy bar
Our love is as precious as a pure diamond
Your kiss sends me into bliss
But, it's just a fantasy

A Tribute Poem To Mary Floyd

I loved to hear you sing the "I Won't Complain" song
Sang it with ease and comfort
I knew you meant every word
I learned a lot about music from you
Loved how you would look me in the face and tell me the truth about myself
Think back to the times you would direct us in the choir
I laugh and remember that time, you said, we sang like "wounded birds"
against the born again choir
I still love "You Said"
You were a musical mom to me
Even when folks called me all sorts of things, you were there to encourage
me
I'll never forget that
Thank God that he allowed you to be in my life
I know that your great voice is leading the heavenly choir now
You may be gone away from me
But nothing will ever take the precious memories
Rest form your labor, Mary
Rest in the arms of Jesus
I know that I will see you one day

Well Done (a poem for Mary, Mildred,Tabitha,Sharon, Pastor Bobo & Walt)

You made it
You're walking them streets of Gold
You're in your mansion
Praising God everyday
Got to hear the master say
Well done my good and faithful servant
Happiness eternal is yours
In a place where love will never die
I'm rejoicing for you
Because you got your two wings
My God told his servant to come home
Well done
Well done
You graduated to the heavenly level
Well done
Servant of the Lord
Well done

I Ain't Scared(poem)

Most people fake,shake & deny themselves
But I ain't scared
They walk around in fear
So scared to be jeered
But I ain't scared
They put on a mask,oh they love to front
But I ain't sacred
Because if you can't accept the real me
Don't need ya anyway
If you don't like what I stand for, Please stay away
On a upward climb
Got no time for lyin'
I ain't scared of your reaction
Not livin' for your satisfaction
You or your god can't stop this
I Ain't scared
No I ain't scared
Try to come against me
And you will see that
I ain't scared to be me

—————————————————

20 Years Ago Today (December5,1993)

20 years ago today, my life was made new
For that was the day, I first accepted you
You wrapped your arms around me
Lord you made me new
My life is so much better because of you
The road hasn't been easy, but the journey
has been worthwhile
Lord you are awesome and to my face, you
bring a smile
My savior and my precious Lord
My best friend, the one who truly understands me
20 years ago, I say I accepted you, but in reality
I became apart of your eternal family
My Lord,my God, thank you for opening your arms to accept me into you salvation's plan
Now with you, I can truly stand
I have joy in my life and in my heart
Now I wanna tell everyone, that in Jesus'(Yeshua's) kingdom they should uniteand be apart
My life is better, because of you Lord
I want to be apart of your for 60 more years
Thank you, Thank you
I thank you Lord, for everything
I thank you for being with me for 20 years
20 years ago today, my life became new, and
it's all because of you.

Lover (POEM)
Most of my friemd's think there's something wrong with me
Cause i'm not hoeing around for a lover
I'm glad that i'm better than that, i'm a different kind of brother
My thinking, is not to force it, let love come to me
So long lasting it will be
Tried to force it in the past and no it didn't work
Ended up dealing with losers and jerks
So i'll wait for my type
the one for me
A true lover, that only wants to be with me
He won't fake in front of his friends
He'll be real 24-7
He'll ake me to cloud 9 and to heaven
He's sure and knows who he is
A real man
That's my ideal lover

It Is What It Is(Poem)

Ain't no use complainin'
I'm just saying
Ain't no use cryin' the blues
Brothers and sisters get some clues
Day by day,work on your solution
Don't let your trials be your conclusion
As I always say,those who complain & expect folks to help them
Will find themselves,alone & needy
Don't be greedy
Life is what you make it
Life hands you challenges to make you a warrior
Simply say to life, you've come to make me strong
So i'll take this, & make it sweet
And It is what it is

Unashamed & Undeafeated(poem)

They tried to make me feel like i'm less than because of where I come from

But I remain unashamed and undefeated
Things have happened in my life
but i'm Unashamed and undeated
Say i'm less than because of who I love
but i'm unashamed and undeated
Try to throw stones because of my economic class
but I stay unshamed and undefeated
I am wonderful just the way I am
The way that I am is amazing
Unequal to anyone else
The way I stride and I step
The way I carry myself
I am unashamed and undefeated by anything or anyone
So I walk with my held high
Unashamed and undeafeated by the cruel world around me

You Turned Me Out (poem)
Delicious thoughts of that night
felt so right,
Climbed the walls in pure pleasure
What am I doing
At the point of no return
Wanna say no
But I simply say yes
High higher, deeper deeper
You are pleasuring me in a new way that I never knew existed
Can't believe I consented to this
Can't believe you turned me out

God Will Supply(poem)
God will supply my every need
Know that for a fact
Never do I doubt that
My faith looks up everyday
My soul and spirit are confident and at rest in every way
Trusting him with every detail of my life
Like Yolanda Adams says it's already alright
What God has for me, no one will take
Every chain he'll break
I'm getting to praisin' to make the enemy mad
I'm joyful, i'm blessed, i'm glad
No matter what I am confident that
God will supply

You Stole My Heart(poem)

You stole my heart,now I want it back
The way you kissed me, the word that you said
The way you loved me
I was helpless in your trap
All you had to do was whisper those sweet words & I was on ya like a dope fiend
Put it on me like no one since my first love had
under your spell,it's too bad
Too bad for me
that i'm in love helplessly

I Wish(poem)

I wish I were Rich
Cause being broke is a bitch
Wish I had a house on Cancoon
I Wish I could be as high as the moon
I Wish I had a fine lover
He would love me like no other
I Wish I had children too
Little me's running around would be cool
I wish this world wasn't so heartless and cruel
I wish we all lived by the golden rule
I wish I were 100% hetero
That would be awesome, you know
I wish all people were free
I wish I could sell a million copies of my books & CDS
But most of all,I wish to be happy now

False Prophet(Rodrick Mayes)(poem)

Should've known you were a wolf in sheep's clothing
All you care about is the dollar
You don't love God's people , you try to pimp then
Hell is reserved for you
You're an undercover homosexual too, that's the worst kind
I should've laid you out when you threatened to beat me up and kill me
You're a punk and an asshole
You're lucky I Haven't called the feds on you, for trying to get me to pay for my ordination
I feel sorry for you church members and everyone who is associated with you
Because you're a false prophet

Nitori ti o ọlọrun(Because Of You God)(poem)

Nitori ti o ọlọrun,mo wa nibi loni(because of you God,I am here today)
Nitori ti o ọlọrun,i jo ki o si kọrin(because of you God, I dance and sing)
Nitori ti o ọlọrun,i gbe ọwọ mi,ki o si yìn o(because of you God,I lift my hands and praise you)
Ifẹ rẹ fun mi ni iyanu(your love for me is amazing)
Mo wa ni iyalenu ti rẹ rere ati aanu si mi(i am in awe of your goodness and mercy to me)
O ṣeun oluwa fun ife mi paapa nigbati mo ko ni ife ara mi (thank you lord for loving me even when i did not love myself)
Ifẹ rẹ jẹ iyanu(your love is wonderful)
Mo ni ife ti o fun ife ati bo mi(i love you for loving and protecting me)
Mo ni ife ti o fun jije ọlọrun loke gbogbo awọn oriṣa(i love you for being God above all gods)
Julọ ga(most high)
Nitori ti o ọlọrun,mo wa nibi loni(because of you God,I am here today)
Nitori ti aanu ati oore rẹ(because of your mercy and grace)
O ṣeun ọlọrun(Thank you God)

One More For The Reader 6

Our 10 year journey is complete
The melody if silence has been sung
Once again,I hope you enjoyed this poetic odysee
Felt my soul
Laughed,cried,reflected
Opened your heart
Until next time, my people
Keep loving,keep living,keep hoping and keep singing

www.ingramcontent.com/pod-product-compliance
Lightning Source LLC
LaVergne TN
LVHW040954150826
845672LV00002B/699
9798230928898